Level Two
(Ages 8+)

Lessons
in
Responsibility
for Boys

(Once-A-Week Curriculum)

This book is dedicated to all the fathers and mothers who diligently seek to train their children in the Lord our God, through the love of Jesus, their Messiah.

PEARABLES

P.O. Box 1071

Mukilteo, WA 98275

www.pearables.com

Instructions

Dear Parent,

We would like to welcome you to our new **Christian Gentleman's Series - Lessons in Responsibility**! So many beloved believers, like yourself, desire with all their hearts that their boys will grow up to be strong men of God. In the world around us we may see many young men who seem to reflect a lack of responsibility in most areas of their lives. These young men will grow up to be tomorrow's adults.

It is our duty as parents to take the time to train young lads in the teachings of our Heavenly Father's Word. The main thing our Savior, Jesus, taught was to first be responsible towards the Father. The first thing in learning responsibility is to teach boys to first, love the Lord their God will ALL their hearts, ALL their souls, ALL their minds, and with ALL their strength. This is what this curriculum is all about. It will instill that loving God first means to be responsible to Him. When they are responsible towards their Heavenly Father, they will then be responsible toward everyone else around them.

This book is a continuation of the first book, Lessons in Responsibility, Volume 1. Its' goal is to have young men consider others before considering themselves. It is a tool to help them rise above themselves and look at what is going on around them.

When using this book, the following suggestions may be of help:

1. This is a once-a-week program. This means that if dad (or mom!) is able to sit down with their son for about one hour a week, the young lad will be able to do the rest of the week's tasks all by himself as he completes his lesson.

2. Please remember to remind your child to continue using his skills which he will have learned the previous weeks. Lessons in Responsibility is just like teaching any other skill. They must practice it again and again and again until it becomes natural to them.

3. Once this book is completed, if you see that your child needs more review in some areas, please feel free to start all over again! Just as reading the Bible only once is never enough, these Biblical and practical suggestions may need to be reviewed again. Don't go on to the next level until you feel your child is ready. It's not about completing a book. It's about having them truly learn and apply the contents of a lesson.

4. Lastly, enjoy this special time with your son. Remember, they grow up so quickly. Smile, laugh and share your joy with him as you learn along with them!

Much love in our Lord and Savior,

PEARABLES

CONTENTS

Jesus said unto him, "Thou shalt love the Lord thy God with ALL thy heart, and with ALL thy soul and with all thy mind, and with all thy strength, this is the first commandment." Mark 12:30

Responsible in Heart

Responsibility

This is Josh. He is Ben's older brother and he has learned a lot about *responsibility*. He is going to help us as we learn what God wants us to be as we grow into gentlemen.

If you haven't yet studied the meaning of responsibility, the Webster's 1828 Dictionary says that it means:

Responsible:

1. Liable to account, accountable; answerable; as for a trust reposed, or for a debt. "We are all responsible for the talents entrusted to us by our Creator."

2. Able to discharge an obligation, or having estate adequate to the payment of a debt.

Responsibility:

1. The state of being accountable or answerable.

Responsibleness:

1. State of being liable to answer, repay or account.

The 1969 American Heritage Dictionary on Responsible:

1. Capable of making moral or rational decisions on one's own and therefore answerable for one's behavior.

2. Able to be trusted or depend upon. Reliable.

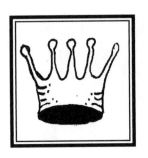

Who are we able to trust and depend upon?____ God first! He is our Creator and our Lord and Savior. We can trust Him for anything we need and for helping us become responsible. We are to walk as He walked. He alone can perfect us and make us into a new creation after we have accepted Jesus Christ as our Lord, our King, our Ruler, our Master who we follow. He alone is our Savior. He can save us from being irresponsible young men!

Can you describe someone who is *irresponsible*? He would be a guy who you can't trust to do what you ask him to do. You wouldn't be able to depend on him for anything!

In one of the definitions we just read, it said that we are all responsible for the talents entrusted to us by our Creator. Talent here didn't mean the word "money" as it did in the following parable, but let's just suppose for a moment that it did. Let's read this with that thought in mind:

"The Kingdom of heaven is as a man traveling into a far country who called his own servants, and delivered unto them his goods.

And unto one he gave five talents, to another, two, and to another one; to every man according to his serval ability; and straightway took his journey.

Then he that received the five talents went and traded with the same, and made them other five talents. And likewise he that had received two, he also gained another two. But he that had received one went and digged in the earth, and hid his Lord's money.

After a long time the Lord of those servants cometh, and reckoneth with them. And so he that had received five talents came and brought other five talents, saying, Lord, thou delivered unto me five talents;

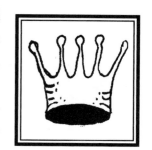

behold, I have gained beside them five talents more. His Lord said unto him, "Well done, thou good and faithful servant; you have been faithful over a few things, I will make thee ruler over many things; enter you into the joy of thy Lord."

He also that had received two talents came and said, "Lord, thou delivered unto me two talents; behold, I have gained two other talents beside them. His Lord said unto him, "Well done, good and faithful servant; you have been faithful over a few things, I will make thee ruler over many things; enter you into the joy of thy Lord."

Then he which had received the one talent came and said, "Lord, I knew thee that thou art an hard man, reaping where thou has not sown, and gathering where thou has now strawed; and I was afraid, and went and hid thy talent in the earth; lo, there thou has that is thine.

His Lord answered and said unto him, "Thou wicked and slothful servant, you knew that I reap where I sowed not, and gather where I have not strawed; you ought therefore to have put my money to the exchangers, and then at my coming I should have received mine own with usury. Take therefore the talent from him, and give it unto him which hath ten talents. For unto every one that hath shall be given, and he shall have abundance; but from him that hath not shall be taken away even that which he has. And cast the unprofitable servant into outer darkness; there shall be weeping and gnashing of teeth. " Matt.25:14-30

Prayer: (In your own words) Ask God to make you responsible so that those around you will see Christ in you. Ask Him to help you be able to be trustworthy and that others will be able to depend upon you.

TASK: Read Matthew 25 each day this week and talk with dad or mom about who was responsible in each of the parables. (Each time you will find something new you didn't see before!)

Hold fast the form of sound words, ... in faith and love which is in Christ Jesus.   2 Timothy 1:13

Week Two

Responsible in Heart

Responsibility - Your Relationship With God First

Josh has decided that he wants to love God with ALL his heart, soul, mind and strength. He memorized Joshua 22:5:

"But take diligent heed to do the commandments and the law, which Moses the servant of the Lord charged you, **To love the Lord your God, and to walk in all His ways, and to keep His commandments, and to cleave unto Him, and to serve Him with all your heart and with all your soul.**"

Our Lord Jesus said the same thing, "The first of all the commandments is, Hear, O Israel; The Lord our God is one Lord. And thou shalt love the Lord thy God with all thy heart, and with all thy soul, and with

all thy mind, and with all thy strength. This is the first commandment." Mark 12: 30

Josh wants more than anything to love God *first* in his life. When you love God first and follow His ways, you will be blessed! God promises this in the Bible.

Did you know that if you reach out to God, He will reach right back out to you and meet you right where you are at? It's true!

The Lord is near unto all them that call upon him, to all that call upon him in truth. He will fulfill the desire of them that fear him; He also will hear their cry and will save them. Psa.145:18,19

And I say unto you, Ask, and it shall be given you; Seek, and you shall find; Knock, and it shall be opened unto you. For every one that asks receiveth; and he that seeks findeth; and to him that knocketh it shall be opened. If a son shall ask bread of any of you that is a father, will he give him a stone? Or if he ask a fish, will he for a fish give him a serpent? Or if he shall ask an egg, will he offer him a scorpion? If you then, being evil know how to give good gifts unto your children; how much more shall your heavenly Father give the Holy Spirit to them that ask him? Luke 11:9+

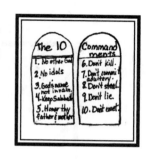

Draw near to God, and he will draw nigh to you.

James 4:8

Behold, I stand at the door and knock. If any man hear my voice, and open the door, I will come in to him, and will sup with him, and he with me. Rev. 3:20

You have a great responsibility towards God. It is to LOVE Him with all your being. Thinking how wonderful, mighty, powerful, merciful and loving He is, it sure isn't a very hard thing to do!

Prayer: (In your own words.) Tell God that you want to learn to love Him with all of your being. Let your heart flow out to Him and ask for His help in loving Him. The Lord wants us to pour out our hearts and ask Him for help. He created us to do this.

TASK: Discuss Deuteronomy 28 with your parents. When you love God and obey Him, is it like obeying your earthly parents? Does God give rules in order to hurt us or to protect us? When you obey your earthly parents are you healthy and happy? When you disobey and walk in the consequences of disobedience, what happens to your quality of life at home?

For the Word of God is quick, and powerful, and sharper than any two edged sword, piercing even to the dividing asunder of soul and spirit, and of the joints and marrow, and is a discerner of the thoughts and intents of the heart. Hebrews 4:12

Week Three

Responsible in Heart

Responsibility & Reading the Bible Consistently

We have a wonderful King who is creating a beautiful place for us right now in His Kingdom. Who is this King? What is He like? Is He a cruel ruler or a just ruler? Is He powerful or does He let others take over? Does He give His subjects freedom or is He a tyrant?

Where do you find these answers about our King? Josh was so curious about our Heavenly Father that he decided to ask his Dad about it. His Dad told him that all the answers could be found in the Bible. This is the only book in the world that will give us true wisdom!

Josh took the Bible his parents gave him and decided that he would read it just like any other book. He started at the beginning in Genesis and read through to the end of Revelation.

He found so many wonderful things about God. He even found that the Bible teaches us that God's Ways are so much higher than ours that we cannot even fathom how great He is. After all, He *is* the Creator of the Universe!

You are old enough now to read the Scriptures without the help of anyone else. Our Heavenly Father wants you to read His Words. The Bible is like a love letter from Him to you. He loves you and wants you to live a life that is worthwhile. God created you for a specific purpose here on earth. You were made for big things, young man!

The Bible will help form your mind, your heart, your body, and your soul. While the rest of the world will tell you many different things, if you are reading the Bible daily, you will be able to say to yourself, "Hey, these guys are saying this..... but the Bible is telling me something else! I think I'll go with what the Bible tells me."

We are in a war. The good side, God's side, wants us to follow Him. Our enemy, the devil, wants us following the prince of this world.

Since you are in a war, you need to have some sort of armour. God wouldn't leave us out here all defenseless, would He? Of course not! Here's what God's Word tells us:

Wherefore take unto you the whole armour of God, that you may be able to withstand in the evil day, and having done all, to stand. Stand therefore, having your loins girt about with *truth*, and having on the breastplate of *righteousness*; and your feet shod with the preparation of the gospel of *peace*, and above all taking the shield of *faith*, wherewith ye shall be able to quench all the fiery darts of the wicked. And take the helmet of *salvation*, and the *sword of the Spirit*, which is the Word of God. Ephesians 6:13-17

Did you notice that all of the armour protects you? Yes! However, God has given you one thing to fight back with ... The SWORD!!!! God's given you a sword! A real one! The Bible tells us here that this sword is the Word of God. How do you sharpen that sword? By knowing the Word of God backwards and forwards. What happens if you let a sword sit for a long time? You forget how to use it. Your sword arm gets flabby and weak and the sword itself will become dull to you. So what is the solution? You must constantly read the Word of God so you will become a master swordsman in the Word of God!

Turn to page 127 to see a daily Bible reading planner that you may want to use.

Prayer: (In your own words) Ask God to help you become responsible towards reading the Word of God daily. Ask Him to help the Word come alive to you and to understand all that you read.

TASK: This week, plan out your own Bible reading schedule. Decide that you will read your Bible daily and map out on a calendar how many chapters you will read. You may want to figure out how long it will take you to read the whole Bible. Then you need to read it again and digest it more and more each time that you go through it. God is living, as is His Word, and He will show you many things as you read it.

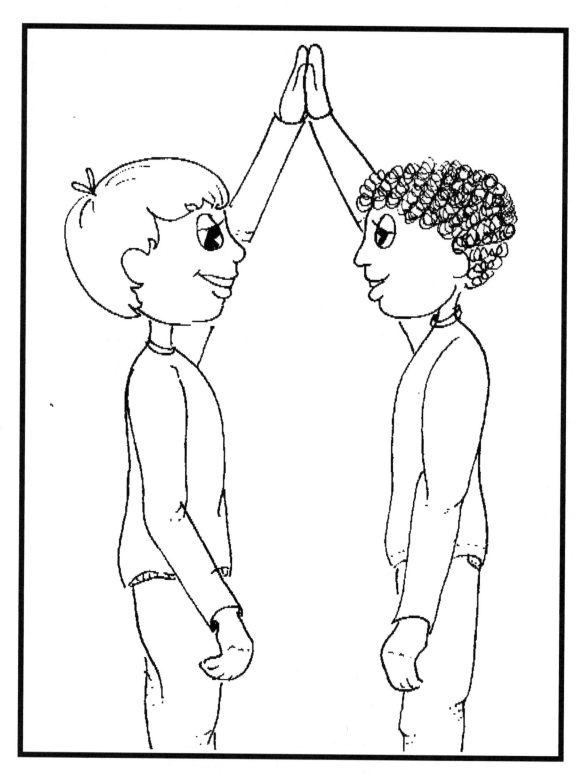

The steps of a good man are ordered by the Lord;
and he delighteth in his way.
Psalms 37:23

Week Four

Responsibility & Fellowship With Other Believers

Josh loves his friends. His friends love God, and because they love God they all help one another to walk in a way that pleases the Lord. When one friend is tempted to do something that isn't right, the other friends say, "Hey! Are you sure you really want to do that. Doesn't the Bible say...?" This is true friendship. It's God's will that we have friends that love us enough to tell us God's truth.

As you are growing up, it is so important that you have friends that are walking in the Lord. The Bible tells us that we are to fellowship with one another. What does *fellowship* mean? The dictionary tells us

that it means:

1. Companionship; society; consort; mutual association of persons on equal and friendly terms. "Have no fellowship with the unfruitful works of darkness." Eph. 5:11

What type of fellowship do you have in your life right now? Do you have fellowship when you go to church? Who are your closest friends? Are they believers in the Lord? Do they help you love God more?

What type of a person are you? Do you help your friends to love God? Do you talk about Him often to them? Do you bring to remembrance different sayings that Jesus teaches us?

Comfort yourselves together, and edify one another, even as also you do. 1 Thess. 5:11

Let us consider one another to provoke unto love and to good works. Not forsaking the assembling of ourselves together as the manner of some is; but exhorting one another. Hebrew 10:24-25

Every day matters in this life. We are either going to live for God and tell others what Jesus says, or we are going to live for ourselves and do our own thing, forgetting our Lord and Savior.

Do we want to have "godless" relationships? A godless relationship is when we get together with others

and never mention God or the Bible. No!!

We want to have "Godly" relationships! This is where we take every opportunity to bring God into our conversations and help others come to know God more closely.

If others around you believe differently, you can still be a light to them. Talk to them about what you read in Scripture. Tell them the neat story about Daniel in the lion's den, David and Goliath, the walls of Jericho... There are hundreds of them. How about Jesus raising the dead? When you start making God a part of your conversation, it will soon become a habit for the friends you are with, too. It will become normal!

Find out in God's Word how you are to behave with your friends. Ask Dad to help you look up some scriptures this week.

Prayer: (In your own words) Talk to Heavenly Father about loving your friends enough to talk to them about Him. Ask Him to show you what to say and to lead you and guide you in all that you do.

TASK: Read the following scriptures this week:

2 Corinthians 6:14-18
Romans 15:1-7
1 Peter 3:8-22
Colossians 3:12-17

For ye were sometimes darkness, but now are ye light in the Lord;
walk as children of light.
Ephesians 5:8

Responsible in Heart

Responsibility & Letting Your Light Shine

Josh just found out that God calls all those who believe in Him a light. Jesus told us, "YOU are the light of the world; a city that is set on a hill cannot be hid. Neither do men light a candle, and put it under a bushel (basket), but on a candlestick; and it gives light unto all that are in the house. Let your light so shine before men, that they may see your good works, and glorify your Father which is in heaven." Matthew 5:14

What does it mean to be a light? Why would you shine? Well, according to this scripture it says to let your light so shine before men, *that they may see your good works*. When they see your good works, then they will glorify your Father which is in heaven.

Wow! Does this mean it matters what you do? What

are good works?

There is a very interesting story that Jesus told to the people. It is about those who DO and those who DON'T do. You've already read this scripture in the very first lesson, but let's review it again:

When the Son of man shall come in his glory, and all the holy angels with him, then shall he sit upon the throne of his glory; and before him shall be gathered all nations; and he shall separate them one from another, as a shepherd divideth his sheep from the goats.

And he shall set the sheep on his right hand, but the goats on the left.

Then shall the King say unto them on his right hand, "Come, ye blessed of my Father, inherit the Kingdom prepared for you from the foundation of the world. For I was an hungred (hungry) and you gave me meat; I was thirsty, and you gave me drink; I was a stranger and you took me in; naked, and you clothed me; I was sick, and you visited me; I was in prison, and you came to me."

Then shall the righteous answer him, saying, "Lord, when did we see thee an hungred, and fed thee? or thirsty, and gave thee drink? When saw we thee a stranger, and took thee in? or naked, and clothed thee? Or when saw we thee sick, or in prison, and came unto thee?"

And the King shall answer and say unto them, "Verily I say unto you, Inasmuch as you have done it unto one of the least of these my brethren, you have done it unto me."

Then shall he say also unto them on the left hand, "Depart from me, ye cursed, unto everlasting fire, prepared for the devil and his angels; for I was an hungred, and ye gave me no meat; I was thirsty, and ye gave me no drink; I was a stranger, and you took me not in; naked, and ye clothed me not; sick, and in prison, and you visited me not."

Then shall they also answer him, saying, "Lord, when saw we thee an hungred, or athirst, or a stranger, or naked, or sick, or in prison, and did not minister unto thee?"

Then shall he answer them, saying, "Verily I say unto you, Inasmuch as ye did it NOT to one of the least of these, ye did it not to me."

And these shall go away into everlasting punishment; but the righteous into life eternal.

What made these sheep DO and what caused the goats NOT to do? It was the state of their hearts. Those who have faith and believe in Jesus have a purpose here on earth. This purpose is to serve our King, our Heavenly Father.

Does doing good works get you in to heaven? No! Doing good works simply shows the faith that you have in your heart. What you DO shows what you BELIEVE.

Prayer: (In your own words.) Ask Father to teach you to be doers of the Word of God and not hearers only. Ask Him to teach you His ways and that He will show you how to walk in them so you will be full of good works.

TASK: Sit down with your parent/s and make a list of things you would like to do that the sheep in Matthew 25 did. Are there ways that you, too, can be full of good works? Discuss with your parents how doing good works will cause men to look at what you are doing and then glorify God. Read this week: Matthew 7:21+, Luke 11:28, James 1:22-27

Execute true judgment, and show mercy and compassions every man to his brother; and oppress not the widow, nor the fatherless, the stranger, nor the poor; and let none of you imagine evil against his brother in your heart. Zechariah 7:9,10

Responsible in Heart

Responsibility & Being a Gentleman for Christ

What is a true "gentleman"? The word "gentleman" in the United States describes a man of good breeding, politeness, and civil manners. The opposite of a gentleman would be a vulgar, clownish and coarse man who has no consideration for others.

Josh had a bad habit when he was younger. He liked to clown around and do foolish things to make other people laugh. He thought this would make his friends like him. Soon his humor turned sour and he started making fun of his friends in order to make them laugh. All it did was make Josh look mean and unkind and soon all his friends backed off and didn't do things with him for awhile.

When he told his Dad about this, his Dad sat him down and talked with him about being polite and thoughtful

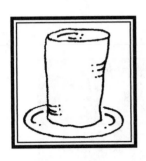

towards others.

The Scriptures tell us that we need to examine ourselves:

Examine yourselves, whether you be in the faith; prove your own selves. Know ye not your own selves, how that Jesus Christ is in you, except ye be reprobates? 2 Corinthians 13:5

Take an honest look at yourself. Are you a gentleman? We'd all like to think of ourselves as perfect. The Bible tells us we all think we are right in our own eyes. But look at yourself as God looks at you.

Are you goofy & sometimes stretch the truth?

Are you clownish? Do you want other people to watch you?

Do you use the good manners your parents have taught you?

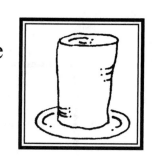

These are questions that every young man must ask himself. When you are learning to become responsible, you must make the decision to become a gentleman. If you want to remain a foolish clown, you will find that you will have fewer and fewer friends as you grow older. Most importantly, you must ask yourself, does God want you to be a fool, or a gentleman for Christ?

Prayer: (In your own words.) Talk to your Heavenly Father and ask him to help you overcome the foolish ways of youth. Ask him to teach you His wisdom and to help you become a gentleman for Christ.

TASK: Read each day one of the following Scriptures this week. Discuss them with your parent/s:

Proverbs 1:7
Proverbs 9:6-8
Proverbs 14:7-9
Matthew 7:24-26
Titus 3:1-7

Charity doth not behave itself unseemly, seeketh not her own...
1 Corinthians 13:5

Week Seven

Responsible in Heart

Responsibility & Being Considerate of Others

Did you know that you may have to learn to think of other people before you think of yourself? Josh has been studying the art of being considerate of others. The opposite of being considerate *is to be selfish*.

The Scriptures have a lot to say about selfishness. One of the most important aspects of being a Christian is that the Lord calls us to DIE to ourselves. Does this mean that we must literally die? Almost. We are supposed to die to ourselves and LIVE IN HIM. We are to get rid of ALL selfishness and only live for our Jesus.

Can *we* do this? Can *we* stop being selfish and put others before ourselves? Yes, but only with Jesus' help!

Let no man seek his own but every man another's wealth. 1 Corinthians 10:24

Look not every man on his own things, but every man also on the things of others. Phillipians 2:4

Josh has been taught a few ways to show consideration for others. Here are a few starter rules:

1. When you are around other people, don't always think of what YOU want to do, but rather ask them what THEY would want to do.

2. Do to OTHERS what you would have them DO to YOU.

3. Give to those who ask from you, and from him that wants to borrow from you do not turn away. Matthew 5:42

4. Be kind to one another, tenderhearted and forgive one another just as God for Christ's sake has forgiven you. Ephesians 4:32

5. Therefore put on, as the elect of God, holy and beloved, bowels of mercies, kindness, humbleness of mind, meekness, longsuffering, forbearing one another, and forgiving one another, if any man have a quarrel against any; even as Christ forgave you, so also do you. Colossians 3:12-13

Prayer: (In your own words.) Ask Father to teach you to be merciful, kind, humble, meek, longsuffering, and forgiving of others quickly. Ask him to help you to never become bitter and to keep your heart soft and pliable for him.

TASK: This week, take a dictionary and with the help of your parent/s look up the following words:

1. Tenderhearted
2. Forgiveness
3. Holy
4. Kindness
5. Humbleness
6. Meekness
7. Longsuffering
8. Forbear and forbearance
9. Consideration
10. Considerate

Let no corrupt communication proceed out of your mouth,
but that which is good to the use of edifying,
that it may minister grace unto the hearers.
Ephesians 4:29

Week Eight

Responsible in Heart

Responsibility & Answering the Phone

In the last lesson we learned a little about being considerate. Showing consideration for others starts at home. There is one invention which brings people into our homes without them even being there. Can you guess what invention this is? Yes, it's the telephone!

Josh had to learn the considerate and polite way of answering and speaking on the phone before his parents would let him use it.

He used to answer, "Hello," while eating a peanut butter sandwich. It sometimes would come out almost like he was speaking another language, "Hug - Yooo." Needless to say, his Dad didn't let him answer the phone again until he started being polite.

Telephone Rules:

1. *Answering the phone:* When answering the phone make sure that you let people know who is on the line. Josh answers the phone like this, "Hello, this is Josh speaking. May I help you?" Or, "Hello, you've reached the Hanson's residence. May I help you?" Always let the other person on the phone know who they are talking to.

2. *When the phone call is for someone other than you and they ask for that person:* Say, "Just a moment please and I will get _____(whoever they are calling for). Put the phone down and go get the person. Do NOT yell for them.

3. *When the person someone is calling for is not at home:* If someone is not at home make sure that you ask the person on the phone who is calling and what their number is. Next, make sure to write down on a piece of paper their name and telephone number and at what time they called.

4. *When you are calling someone:* Make sure that you always give your name when you are calling. Josh would say, "Hello, Mr. Thompson. This is Josh. May I please speak to Jimmy?" If you know who has

answered the phone, always say hello to him first as shown in this example.

5. *Leaving a message on an answering machine:* The polite thing to do when you get an answering machine is to leave a message. Leave your name, the reason you are calling, the time you are making the call, and your telephone number so he may return the call. Josh's message would sound something like this: "Hello, Jimmy. This is Josh Hanson calling. It's about 2:00 and I was calling to see if you would like to go to a basketball game this Friday. Please call me back at 555-5555."

6. *Things you should never, ever do:* Do not ever make prank jokes using the telephone. This can lead to trouble with the police. Do not listen in to other people's conversations. Do not talk to someone else when you are on the phone. Do not stay on the phone too long or keep someone else on too long by talking too much.

Prayer: (In your own words.) Ask the Lord to help you learn how to be kind and considerate on the phone. Ask him to remind you that you are being a light even when you are using the telephone.

TASK: Sit down with your parents and ask them how they would like you to answer the phone in your home. Ask them if you may practice this week by answering the phone calls in your house. In the beginning

A man that has friends must show himself friendly; and there is a
friend that sticketh closer than a brother.
Proverbs 18:24

Week Nine

Responsible in Heart

Responsibility & Introducing Others

Josh has many friends. Sometimes he invites different friends over at the same time that do not know each other.

Other times he sees new people at church and wants to introduce a new fellow to his friends. At first he was a bit nervous and didn't really know what to say until his Dad taught him how to introduce people to each other. It was really very simple and was another way to be a light in God's Kingdom.

Let's use an example of a situation that happened to Josh. Josh saw a new guy his age in his Church Class. He looked like a really nice person and Josh could see that the fellow was a bit lonely and kind of nervous. During the class there really wasn't time to go over and introduce himself so he waited until it was finished.

Step 1. He went up to the boy and said to him,

"Hello, my name is Josh Hanson. What is your name?"

Step 2. The boy looked back at him and said, "Hi, my name is Todd Parker."

Step 3. Josh repeated his name so he would remember later. "Hi, Todd Parker! It's very nice to meet you. Welcome to our church class."

Step 4. Josh didn't stop there. If he would have, he wouldn't be able to really get to know Todd. He asked five questions that his Dad had taught him to ask someone new.

1. Are you new here?
2. How old are you?
3. What grade are you in?
4. What is your favorite sport to play?
5. Would you like to meet some of my friends?

Step 5. When Josh introduced Todd to his other two friends, he took Todd with him and said, "Hi, James and Brian. I want you to meet Todd Parker." Then he turned to Todd and said, "Todd these are my friends James and Brian."

Remember, the most important thing to a person is their name. Always remember to use it!

Prayer: (In your own words.) Talk to our Heavenly Father and tell Him how you want to help new people feel comfortable when they are at church or in your home. Ask Him to help you show His love and kindness to everyone you meet.

TASK: This week, make an effort to introduce two people that do not know each other. If you can't think of anyone, then ask your parents to help you with this task. Try it at church or in your home. Invite two friends over who do not know each other. It is your duty to make sure that both friends are introduced to each other and that they become comfortable in your home as they play together with you.

Set a watch, O Lord, before my mouth;
keep the door of my lips.
Psalms 141:3

Week Ten

Responsible in Mind

Responsibility & How to Interact With Others

Did you know that we have to be taught how to interact with others? It's true. If you lived in the jungle and you were brought up by apes, you would probably be like Tarzan and jump up and down and hit your chest when you didn't like something.

Since we know you weren't brought up by monkeys, let's talk a bit about how God might like us to interact and behave around other people.

There are times when we are going to be around friends or family and we won't have a clue of what to say to them. Sometimes, we may pull a blank and then say silly things just to fill in the gap. That's OK. It happens to everybody.

Here are some suggestions of things to talk about that may help you in these sticky situations.

1. *Always talk about the other person.* If you are in a room with people and you are left talking to one person, it is so easy to just ask questions. Find out more about them. Ask them what they like, what their favorite sport, hobby, subject or animal is. Ask them about their families.

2. *Ask them what church they go to.* If they do not go to a church you can talk to them about what they have read in the Bible. If they haven't read the Bible, you have a great opportunity to tell them some of the things that you know about God.

3. *Things NOT to talk about:* Never tell jokes that are coarse, dirty, about different cultures, or that would make our Jesus unhappy. Do not ever, ever talk about other people. This is called gossip and should always be avoided. Do not say negative or bad things about food, places, or anything! Keep positive. Show the love of Jesus.

Prayer: (In your own words.) Ask Father God to help you always be kind to everyone. Ask for His help to always keep your communication with people pleasing to Him. Confess things that you have done (like being mean, hurting others, not sharing, etc.,) to our Heavenly Father and tell Him that you need His help to say the right things and show His love to others.

TASK: This week make it a goal to talk to at least two new people that you do not know very well. Make them feel comfortable and learn all you can about them. When you come home, sit down with Dad or Mom and tell them what you learned and what you did during your conversation.

And Jesus lifted up his eyes, and said, "Father, I thank thee that thou hast heard me. And I knew that thou hearest me always; but because of the people which stand by I said it, that they may believe that thou hast sent me."

John 11:41-42

Lesson Eleven

Responsible in Mind

Responsibility & How to Really Listen & Hear

Josh is one of the best listeners you will ever find. He didn't always have this attribute. Something happened one day that changed him and he has been a great listener ever since.

Here's his story... One day Josh was sitting at the breakfast table and his mother said something to him. He couldn't quite hear what she said over the crunch he was making as he chewed his Crispy Oats. Rather than asking her to repeat what she said, he continued on reading his cereal box and eating his breakfast.

His mom came back in the room and said something to him again. He was sure that she was reminding him to do one of his chores, so he decided to just ignore her and continued on eating.

His mother, seeing that he was still eating, asked in a loud voice, "OK, Josh?"

Josh nodded his head and went on chewing his food and reading the cereal box even though he hadn't heard a word she'd said.

Later that day there was a knock on the door. His good friend from the neighborhood had come over to see if he could play baseball in the back field.

He went to ask his mother for her permission to go.

"Sure, Josh. As long as you folded the clothes I asked you to fold this morning. Did you do your chore?"

Josh shook his head. He hadn't listened to his mother, so he wasn't able to go out and play baseball that day.

****

God wants us to listen to our parents.

"Now therefore hearken (listen) unto me, O ye children; for blessed are they that keep my ways. Hear instruction, and be wise, and refuse it not. Blessed is the man that heareth me, watching daily at my gates, waiting at the posts of my doors. For whoso findeth me findeth life, and shall obtain favor of the Lord." Proverbs 8:32-36

Also, " A wise son heareth his father's instruction; but a scorner heareth not rebuke." Proverbs 9:1

What did you understand from these two scriptures?_____ What does God want you to hear? Instruction! You are to keep your ears open for the instruction of the Lord and your parent's instruction.

Here is another Scripture that you should memorize this week:

"Wherefore, my beloved brethren, let every man be swift to hear, slow to speak, slow to wrath; for the wrath of man worketh not the righteousness of God." James 1:19-20

God wants us to keep our ears open and our mouths slow to speak. In other words, we must think before we speak.

Here are some suggestions on listening:

1. When someone speaks to you, give them your attention.

2. Look them straight in the eye to show you are listening.

3. After they have said something to you, respond back so they know you have heard them.

Prayer: (In your own words.) Ask the Lord to make you a hearer and a listener.

TASK: Read the following Scriptures this week:
Luke 6:47-49
Matthew 13:14-23
Romans 2:13

He died for all, that they which live should not henceforth live unto
themselves, but unto him which died for them, and rose again."
2 Corinthians 5:15

Week Twelve

Responsible in Mind

Responsibility & Centering On Others, Not Self

Have you ever been around a truly selfish person? The Bible tells us in the last days there will be many people who will be **lovers of their own selves**, covetous, boasters, proud, blasphemers, disobedient to parents, unthankful, unholy, without natural affection, trucebreakers, false accusers, incontinent, fierce, despisers of those that are good, traitors, heady, high-minded, lovers of pleasures more than lovers of God, having a form of godliness, but denying the power thereof... from such people turn away. 2 Timothy 2:2-5

Boy, this doesn't sound very pleasant, does it? You can't really do much about other people who are this way, but you can sure ask our Heavenly Father to help you so that you aren't any of those things.

Josh calls it "turning the self button off". He starts to think about himself and then says, "No way!" and thinks of how other people might feel.

Did you know Josh is very, very happy? You become happy when you think of other people. Not only are you happy, but you are living out what God wants you to do. Remember what we learned in a previous lesson? We are to DIE to ourselves, and LIVE in Christ!

Rules for living a "OTHER-centered" (not self-centered) life:

1. Don't talk about yourself all the time. Say a little bit and then listen to others.

2. Don't be the only one to make decisions. Let other people have a say about things.

3. Don't be bossy. Ask rather than tell.

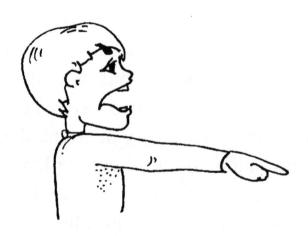

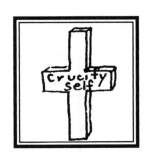

4. Don't brag. This means bragging about something that you have that others might not, or someplace you've been that others have not.

5. Don't make fun of others trying to make yourself look better. Only speak things that are uplifting and pleasant and make your friends feel comfortable.

Prayer: (In your own words.) Talk to Father about becoming unselfish. Tell Him that you don't want to be selfish at all; you want to let Jesus live in you. Ask Him for His Holy Spirit to guide you in all that you do and say.

TASK: Sit quietly with your parents and discuss with them if you have a problem with "self" sometimes. Pray with them and ask them to help you when the "selfish bug" comes out and gets you. Read the Scriptures: John 3:3-16 ; Romans 6:2

And having food and raiment (clothing) let us be content.
1 Timothy 6:8

Week Thirteen

Responsible in Mind

Responsibility & How Your Clothes Show Who You Are

Have you noticed how everyone has a uniform of some sort? It's true. Skateboarders have certain clothes they wear, snowboarders wear certain clothes, hikers have certain clothes, businessmen wear certain types of clothing. Our clothing represents who we are... what we like.

Let's talk about how we appear to other people. When someone first comes up to you for the first time, they get was is called "a first impression". First impressions are very important.

Josh had an interesting experience with first impressions. He had been out playing all day in the back yard

and was totally dirty. He looked like he hadn't taken a bath for days.

Some new friends from church stopped by the house and brought their children for Josh and his brothers and sisters to meet.

Their first impression of Josh was that his hair was very dirty, his face smudged with mud, his clothes were filthy and torn in places. Later on, after they had all become good friends, one of the boys told him that they had thought he was a messy, someone who didn't like to be clean! This was because of his first impression.

Remember that we are representatives for our Savior, Jesus! We are God's ambassadors. This doesn't mean we have to dress like royalty even though our Heavenly Father is a King. It does mean that we should take care of what God has given us.

Here's some suggestions for every day dress:

1. *Make sure that your clothes are clean and smell nice.*

2. *Wear colors that match.* For example don't wear bright green stripes with purple plaid pants.

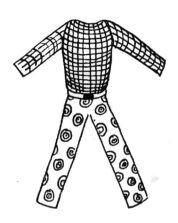

3. *If your clothes are wrinkled, ask Mom or sister to iron it.* (You can learn how to do it yourself when you are a little older).

4. *Once you are dressed, stand tall.* Do not slouch or slump over your shoulders. Lift up your head and do not let your head hang down to your chest.

Prayer: (In your own words.) Thank your Heavenly Father for the clothing He's given you to wear. Ask Him to help you treat all the blessings that He's given, in a good manner. Ask Him to help you be observant of those who may need your clothing once you grow out of them.

TASK: This week spend some time in your room organizing your clothing according to what goes with what. You can either do this by hanging them up in a closet or folding them in your drawers. Ask Dad or Mom for help if you need it.

He that overcometh, the same shall be clothed in white raiment, and I will not blot out his name out of the book of life, but I will confess his name before my Father and before his angels.
Revelation 3:5

Week Fourteen

Responsible in Mind

Responsibility & What to Wear When

The Scripture on the previous page is very interesting. Did you know that in Heaven the Lord will give us clothes to wear? They will be white and they will be made by God. White stands for purity and holiness.

Josh knows that he has to wear certain clothes during the week. For church, or special occasions, he will have another set of clothes to wear. When we are in heaven, we are going to have our Heavenly set of clothes that our Father wants us to wear.

Josh is going to a wedding. One day before the wedding, he pulled out his blue jeans and a white shirt. He sometimes wore this to church. When he went downstairs to show his Mom looked horrified.

"Josh! You can't wear clothing like that to a wedding."

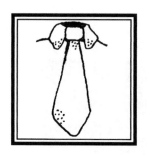

Josh felt embarrassed because he didn't know what else to wear. His Dad and Mom quickly showed him some clothes that he had worn for a funeral. He learned that it didn't matter whether you died or got married, you wore the same type of clothes!

Here's some helpful tips:

1. Always wear nice dress pants and a white buttoned down shirt with a tie and jacket to a wedding, a funeral, a Bar Mitzvah (a young man's coming of age - for Jewish or Christian ceremonies), or fancy party. *This is called formal dressing.*

2. When going to a nice restaurant, Holiday meal or celebration, wear a nice pair of dress pants and a nice shirt that either buttons down or has some type of collar and a tie. *This is called casual dressing.*

3. When working, wear old pants and older T-shirts that can get torn or stained.

4. Daily wear: You can wear anything your Dad and Mom want you to wear. Usually kids wear clean pants and a matching clean shirt.

Prayer: (In your own words.) Ask Father to help you glorify Him in all that you do. Also ask Him to help you keep a humble heart and to never be vain.

TASK: This week, ask your parents to help you organize your formal or casual clothes in your closet. They should be hung up and ready to be worn for special occasions.

Read the Scriptures in Luke 12:22-31

Let your moderation be known to all men.
Philippians 4:5

Week Fifteen

Responsibility & Being a Modest Gentleman

Josh went to the mall with his parents the other day. He saw some boys who were about nine or ten all dressed up in very different clothing that he had never seen anyone wear before.

They had black clothing on which had tears and cuts all down the pant legs. Their black T shirts were all sprayed with red spray paint and their hair was sticking straight up.

After Josh saw the young men he asked his parents if he could wear clothing like that too.

His father told him that he would talk to him about it when he got home from the mall. This is what his Dad said...

"I understand that you liked the clothing that those

Real Men Wear Manly Clothes!

boys were wearing. As a believer in Christ, you need to ask yourself the following questions when you decide to dress yourself:

1. Would Jesus wear this?
Jesus is the gentleman of all gentlemen. If you cannot imagine Jesus wearing an item of clothing, then you shouldn't wear it.

2. Would this be modest?
Modest means that you are not calling attention to yourself. When you wear clothing that shouts, "Look at me!" the clothing is not modest.

3. Is this extreme in any way?
Extreme means to go too far one way. The Bible tells us that we should let our moderation be known to all men. Philippians 4:5. What is moderation? According to the dictionary moderation means: 1. To restrain from excess of any kind. To be temperate; observing reasonable bounds of indulgence.

4. What would be my friends' first impression if they saw me wearing this?
If your friends would gasp or make a comment on your clothing for its strangeness, then you are not wearing clothes that a gentleman would wear.

5. What is my motive for wearing this?
Why are you choosing to wear something? For

attention? To make a statement? Are you making a statement for Christ of modesty and holiness?

6. Is it too costly?

Remember the Scriptures which talk about not spending too much money on clothing or jewels or adornment. This goes for both men and women. Some name brands are four times the cost of a regular T-shirt simply because they have the name of a famous designer on the front. Then we unknowingly advertise their products, and pay to do so!"

Ask yourself these questions when you get tempted to go "way out" with your clothing. Remember that you are a gentleman. Dress accordingly.

Prayer: (In your own words.) Ask Heavenly Father to remind you to not store up your treasures on earth but rather to store up things in heaven. If you are picky about your clothing, ask God to help you with this problem. Again, be thankful for all the clothing and items that your Heavenly Father has given you. Always thank Him for what you have.

TASK: Discuss with your father how "real men" dress. Look at how your father dresses and copy him. He is a *real man*! Talk with your dad about the different styles there are for men and ask him what he thinks would be appropriate to wear.

What? Know ye not that your body is the temple
of the Holy Ghost which is in you, which ye have of God,
and ye are not your own?
1 Corinthians 6:19

Week Sixteen

Responsible in Strength

Responsibility & A Nicely Groomed Gentleman

You have already learned so much about what to wear, when to wear it, but now there is one more thing to talk about regarding your outward appearance.

Are you well groomed?

"Well groomed?" you ask.

Being well groomed means that a man has taken the time to maintain and care for himself. Take a look at your Dad. I bet his hair is cut nicely and washed. His nails are probably clipped just right. His ears are free from ear wax. His teeth are brushed and flossed daily. He smells good because he wears deodorant and after shave. These are all the things a man does to take care of himself daily.

Now you may not need to shave or wear deodorant yet, but you do need to keep your hair, face, ears and nails clean.

Here's some hygiene steps for you to follow if you have forgotten from the Level One book:

1. Hair: Make sure to shampoo and scrub your scalp with your fingers when you wash. This eliminates dandruff and dry scalp. Use conditioner. You should wash your hair every two days.

2. Face: Take a washcloth, lather it up with soap, and scrub in a circular motion all over your face, behind your ears and the front and back of your neck. This should be done daily, if not more.

3. Ears: You may want Dad or Mom to help you with this the first time. Take an ear cleaner pipe (the type with cotton at both ends) and gently go around the inside of your outer ears in gentle circles, keeping the cotton turning carefully. Do not go into the ear canal as you could damage your ears. This should be done once or twice a week.

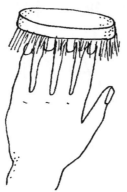

4. Nails: Scrub your nails with a nail brush in between clippings. Have Dad show you how to clip your nails straight across. You should do this once a week.

Prayer: (In your own words.) Thank Father God for your health. Ask Him to help you do your part to keep your body clean and healthy.

TASK: Ask Dad to show you how to properly complete each portion of your hygiene steps. This week make sure to groom (clean) every listed portion of your body. (Don't forget your daily bath!)

Let a man so account of us, as of the ministers of Christ, and stewards of the mysteries of God. Moreover it is required in stewards, that a man be found faithful.   1 Corinthians 4:1

Week Seventeen

Responsible in Strength

Responsibility & Being a Good Steward

God wants us to be good stewards of the things He gives us. The dictionary tells us that a steward is a manager for a high Lord. We are stewards for our High Lord, our King and Heavenly Father.

What would He like us to manage? Everything that He has given us. However, in this week's lesson we are going to discuss how to be good stewards or managers of our money.

The Bible tells us that Jesus told his disciples that there was a certain rich man, which had a steward. This steward was accused unto him that he had wasted his goods.

And he called him, and said to him, "How is it that I hear this of you? Give an account of your steward-ship; for you may no longer be steward."

Then the steward said within himself, "What shall I do? For my Lord takes away from me the stewardship. I cannot dig. I am ashamed to beg. I am resolved what to do, that when I am put out of the stewardship, they may receive me into their houses."

So he called every one of his Lord's debtors unto him, and said unto the first, "How much do you owe to my Lord?"

And he said, "A hundred measures of oil."

And he said to him, "Take your bill, and sit down quickly, and write fifty."

Then said he to another, "And how much do you owe?"

And he said, "A hundred measures of wheat."

And he said to him, "Take your bill, and write forty."

And the Lord commended the unjust steward, because he had done wisely; for the children of this world are in their generation wiser than the children of light."

Luke 16:1-8 (our paraphrase)

The Lord goes on to say that the person that is faithful in that which is least is faithful also in much; and he that is unjust in the least is unjust also in much. If therefore you have not been faithful with the unrighteous riches, who will commit to your trust the true riches? And if you have not been faithful in that which is another man's, who shall give to you your own?

What do you think these Scriptures mean? We are to be faithful with the things that God has given us. You need to learn to be wise with the money that God will give you.

When you grow up to be a man and have a job that earns money, you must learn how to handle the money. Do you remember how to divide your money up? Remember in the last book, Ben had learned to give 10% to God. You place half of the remaining amount and put it into your savings bank. The rest you may spend if you like.

Prayer: (In your own words.) Tell the Lord how thankful you are that He provides everything that we need. Ask Him for wisdom and guidance as you become a steward for Him. Tell Him you want to learn how to handle His gifts wisely starting right now.

TASK: It is very important that you learn to handle your money wisely. You don't have any money to handle? This week find jobs that you can do to start making some money to manage. You can go around your neighborhood and offer to weed people's yards. You can rake leaves in the fall. You can run errands for those who can't. Sit with your Dad and Mom and ask them to help you come up with ways to earn some income. A great book to read is: Economics for Kids - go to www.BluestockingPress.com.

But whoso hath this world's good, and seeth his brother have need, and shutteth up his bowels of compassion from him, how dwelleth the love of God in him? My little children, let us not love in word, neither in tongue; but in deed and truth.
1 John 3:17

Week Eighteen

Responsible in Strength

Responsibility & A "Give Me" Heart

Josh had some trouble a while back. He had what his Dad called a "Give Me" heart. Over time this was shortened to a "Gimme" heart. Josh just had a very hard time when it came to wanting things. He didn't want to share, he didn't want to listen to other people. He just wanted everything given to him and never thought of giving to other people.

One day, his Dad took him to a Bible study where they were talking about how here in America we have everything we need. They showed pictures of children his age who lived with dirt floors and who didn't even have water to drink. They didn't have shirts on their backs and some of their parents had died from lack of

food. Something happened that day to Josh's heart. The Holy Spirit really changed that "give me" heart.

Please
Holy Spirit
Fill My
Heart

He wanted to DO something to help those children. At the Bible Study there was an organization which helped those people. You could sign up and pay $15 each month and help to sponsor a child. Josh was so excited! He asked his Dad if he could do this and his Dad was more than happy to say yes.

From that time on Josh became thankful for the things that he has. He works at odd jobs around the neighborhood in order to earn the money each month. Surprisingly, that $15 is usually the 10% he puts away for his giving money (tithe). The Lord blesses him with a great income each month!

Now Josh has his sponsor child's picture on his refrigerator and prays for him daily.

Do you have a "Give me" heart? Do you want everything given to you? Really be honest with yourself. If you feel that you, too, have a "give me" heart, all you have to do is to go to your Heavenly Father and ask Him to help you. He will!

Prayer: (In your own words.) Thank Heavenly Father for all your worldly goods he has given you. Ask Him to help you to have a generous and loving heart towards everyone. Ask Him to always teach you about true treasure and not just earthly.

TASK: This week you have a project to complete:

1. Take a list of paper and go throughout your house and write down on a numbered list, everything that you own. This will take you a very long time, but do it throughout the week.

2. Next, take that list and ask yourself how you take care of (are you a good steward) of all the things on the list? Write good, little, or bad next to the items.

3. Pray with Dad and Mom and thank God for all that He has given you using the list in front of you.

4. Make another list of all the things you want (this is for the "Give Me" monster in us).

5. Ask yourself if you NEED these things in order to live, or just WANT these items because of that little *Give me Monster* in you. Could you take the money that you would spend on your wants and give it to the poor?

6. Read: Psalms 112:5, 9, Prov. 13:7, Luke 6:38

To do good and to communicate (be a benefactor) forget not, for with such sacrifices God is well pleased. Hebrews 13:16

Week Nineteen

Responsible in Strength

Responsibility & A Giving Heart

In last week's lesson we told the story of how God changed Josh's heart. Now he loves to give to others in any way he can.

Our Mighty King wants us to give part of the money that we have to the poor. There are some people who look down at the poor and make fun of them and despise them. God does not want us to have this ugly attitude towards anyone. Remember the Scripture about the Sheep and the Goats? Jesus said, "If you have done it to the least of these, you have done it unto me." When we give, we are giving to Jesus. We need to love each person that is hurting and poor as if that person were Jesus Himself.

Most of the world looks at those of us who live in America as if we are rich. Compared to many of the other countries, we are rich. But being rich, we have a responsibility to others:

Charge them that are rich in this world, that they be not high-minded, nor trust in uncertain riches, but in the living God, who giveth us richly all things to enjoy. That they do good, that they be rich in good works, ready to distribute, willing to communicate. Laying up in store for themselves a good foundation against the time to come, that they may lay hold on eternal life. 1 Timothy 6:17-19

What are we commanded to do here? How should you live your life? Let's make some steps!

Step 1: We are to do good and be rich in good works.

Step 2: We are to be ready to distribute (money, food, etc.)

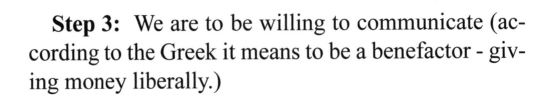

Step 3: We are to be willing to communicate (according to the Greek it means to be a benefactor - giving money liberally.)

Step 4: Every day we must get on our knees before the Lord our God and thank Him for all that He has given us.

Prayer: (In your own words.) Thank Heavenly Father for all our blessing in this earth. Ask Him to keep our minds on heaven and to keep us from being choked by the riches and cares of this world. Ask Him to keep our hearts and minds and souls only on Him and to show us ways to help those who are in need. Ask Him to remind us to always be aware of other's needs.

TASK: This week there are a number of tasks to complete:

1. Go online or go to an encyclopedia and look up the country Uganda. Look up information regarding their culture and see how these people live. You can do it with any country such as Columbia, Bolivia. Compare their way of life with your own. Would you say you are rich?

2. Discuss with Dad and Mom how you can help someone with your "giving money" (tithe). You may want to sponsor a child. You can do this through Compassion International * 3955 Cragwood Dr. * Colorado Springs, CO * 80933. There are many other ways to help others. Maybe someone in your own family. A neighbor, someone in your church or Bible Study. Pray with your parents for wisdom and guidance, but don't forget to give. Read: 2 Cor. 8:7-14; 9:6-13; Matt. 6:1-4

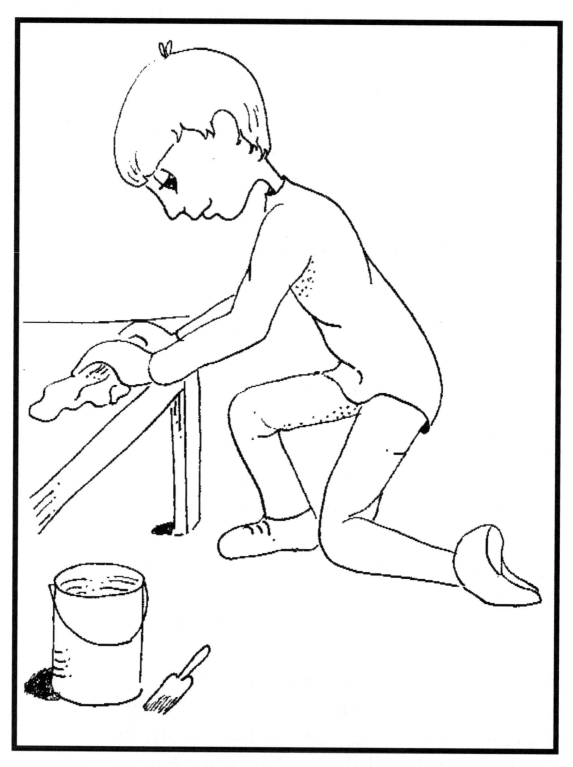

If any provide not for his own, and specially for those of his own
house, he hath denied the faith, and is worse than an infidel.
1 Timothy 5:8

Week Twenty

Responsible in Strength

Responsibility & Being a Hard Worker

This is a picture of the new Josh. This is after he learned how to work hard and stopped being.... lazy. Now lazy is not a very nice word, is it? The Bible calls it being slothful. When you are slothful it means that you are not doing anything. You just sit around and watch as life goes by, never doing anything useful. Do you know what a sloth is? It is an animal that barely moves.

God tells us that the soul of a sluggard desires or wants but will never have anything. It also tells us that slothfulness casts the sloth into a deep sleep; and that an idle soul shall suffer hunger. It says that a slothful person's desires kill him, for his hands refuse to work but yet he covets greedily all the day long! Proverbs 13:4, 19:15; 21:25-26. (our paraphrase)

Wow! That is a very lazy person. At one time, Josh thought that it was a bad thing to work. He thought that work was punishment. He had it all wrong. Work is a great thing!

Did you know that the Bible teaches us in the book of Genesis that before evil ever came into the world, Adam was given work to do? Yep! His job was to dress and keep the garden. Genesis 2:15 He was the first farmer!

Work isn't a punishment. Work is what we were created for. God worked six days and then rested one and made the Sabbath Holy.

The Bible gives us everything that we need to know to live productive, happy lives.

Here are some rules that Scripture says to follow regarding work:

Rule 1: Be DILIGENT in all that you do. (See you a man diligent in his business? He shall stand before kings; he shall not stand before mean men. Prov.22:29)

Rule 2: Do your job with ALL YOUR MIGHT. (Whatsoever thy hand findeth to do, do it with thy might; for there is no work, nor device, nor knowledge, nor wisdom, in the grave, whither thou goest. Eccl. 9:10)

Rule 3: Be FERVENT in Spirit in all that you do, not slothful. (Not slothful in business; fervent in spirit; serving the Lord. Romans 12:11)

Rule 4: Be quiet as you work, do your own business, work with your own hands. (Study to be quiet, and to do your own business, and to work with your own hands, as we commanded you. 1 Thess. 4:11)

Rule 5: **Work knowing that you are going to help others that are in need of any excess that you have.** (That you may walk honestly toward them that are without, and that ye may have lack of nothing. 1 Thess. 4:12)

Rule 6: **Trust God that He says that you will never lack for anything if you live this way.** (1 Thess 4:12)

Prayer: (In your own words) Ask the Lord to help you to be a hard worker. Ask him to remove anything that is lazy or idle in you. Tell Him that you want to do all things for Him and that you want to have a generous and giving Spirit.

TASK:

1. Take some time this week to look up on the internet or in the dictionary or encyclopedia the definition of what a sloth is.

2. With Dad or Mom, look up the following words in the dictionary:

Diligent

Might

Fervent

Trust

3. Discuss with your Dad how he works and what is expected of him at his job. You can learn so much

Be not among winebibbers; among riotous eaters of flesh; for the
drunkard and the glutton shall come to poverty;
and drowsiness shall clothe a man with rags.
Proverbs 23:20-21

Week Twenty-One

Responsible in Strength

Responsibility & Handling Your Money Wisely

We've already touched just a bit on handling your money, but you are getting so responsible that you are now able to understand a little bit more!

Josh just learned that his money can grow! Have you ever heard the saying that "money doesn't grow on trees"? Well, this is true. But money *can* grow in a bank, in a savings account.

Do you remember how much you are supposed to put into your savings account? After you receive your money that you earn, you put 10% in a giving account (tithe). Next, you take half of what is left and place that in a savings account. The rest you may spend on your needs.

In this lesson we are going to learn about opening a savings account. It is different than your piggy bank. A savings account at a bank or credit union pays you to use the money that you place in the bank. The wise stewards in the Scriptures took their money and invested it. So should we be wise with our money. Rather than let our money just sit, we can let our money make more for us.

Step 1: Ask your parents to take you down to their bank. Also ask them if a savings account there pays the most interest on a savings account. Interest is the amount of money you are going to get from the bank by letting them use your savings.

Step 2: Once you are at the bank, fill out the forms that you will need to sign. Give them the money that you have been saving. Now it will start making more money for you! Take the papers that they give you and place them in a safe place in your room.

Step 3: Every time you get paid for your work,

calculate your savings amount and take it to the bank. Your money will keep doubling.

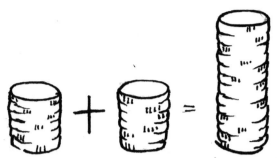

Step 4: Watch for your bank statement in the mail. It will tell you how much money you are earning by placing your savings in the bank.

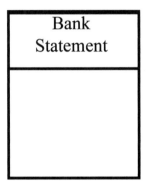

Prayer: (In your own words.) Ask Heavenly Father to make you wise and to give you self-control. Self-control is one of the fruits of having His Spirit.

TASK: Discuss with your parents what you should do with your money that you want to spend. You might even want to think about putting that money into your savings account. You can always draw it out when you need it. Read: Matthew 25: 15-28 again. Talk to Dad about investing your money in something that will make you money... This will prepare you for the next book.

Be thou diligent to know the state of thy flocks,
and look well to thy heards.
Proverbs 27:23

Week Twenty-Two

Responsible in Strength

Responsibility At Home

Josh loves his family. He likes his home, his room, his brothers and sisters. He is so thankful that God gave him his family.

Josh has learned so much about work and helping others at home. He takes turns helping with his brothers to maintain their home and keep it in top shape. If he and his brothers do not maintain their house and yard, it will soon decay and crumble, and weeds will take over the yard.

When God gives you a home it is your responsibility to take care of what He has given you.

Do you help take care of your home? Do you have responsibilities that you must do because you are a member of your family?

Maybe you and Josh have the same responsibilities?

Here is a list of chores that Josh has:

1. Help wash the car
2. Vacuum, sweep & mop
3. Dust wood with polish and use feather duster
4. Take care of pet, walk and feed the dog
5. Empty the wastebaskets on garbage day
6. Fold and put away laundry
7. Clean the tub and sinks with cleanser & sponge
8. Make bed and clean up room
9. Prepare an easy breakfast
10. Clear the kitchen table after meals
11. Rinse and put dishes in the dishwasher
12. Weed the lawn & flower gardens
13. Rake leaves and put them in bags
14. How to water the lawn

Do you have different chores and responsibilities? Just remember the lesson that we learned regarding working hard. We need to be *diligent*!

Remember that when you are diligent you are looking at your job and working carefully and consistently. You are concentrating on the task at hand and not distracted from your job. You do not stop until the task is completed. There is a smile on your face and a song in your heart.

Josh's little brother, Ben, had a chore chart that he and his Dad made. Since you have a lot more chores than he did, why don't you concentrate on making up a chart that will help you get your chores in order.

It might look something like this:

CHORE LIST
1
2
3
4
5
6
7
8

	Mon	Tues	Wed	Thur	Fri	Sat
Clean Tub & Sinks	X			X		
Vacuum Bedroom		X				
Sweep and Dust House		X				
Make Breakfast	X		X		X	
Kitchen Duty		X		X		X
Room Cleaned & Bed made	X	X	X	X	X	X
Take garbage out			X			
Put dishes away in dishwasher		X		X		X
Fold & put away laundry					X	
Water lawn			X		X	
Feed & walk the Dog	X	X	X	X	X	X
Do Yard Work						X

Prayer: (In your own words.) Ask our Father to help you be consistent and to do your chores with a cheerful and helpful heart. Tell Him that you don't want to complain but that you want to help around your home.

TASK: This week, organize your chore list and see if you can complete all your jobs with care and consistency. Consistency means that you make your chores a habit and do a great job. Sit with your parents and ask them to help you write down all the chores that you need to be responsible for. Read: Proverbs 24:30-34; 26:13-16; 2 Thessalonians 3:10-11; Proverbs 12:27

Put on therefore, as the elect of God, holy and beloved,
bowels of mercies, kindness, humbleness of mind, meekness, longsuffering; and above all these things, put on charity, which is the
bond of perfectness.
Colossians 3:12, 14

Week Twenty-Three

Responsible in Strength

Responsibility & How to Rake Leaves

Raking leaves is a very big and important job that needs to be done every year. Have you already had the opportunity to learn how to rake leaves? There are two ways to rake leaves.

Josh has learned both ways of raking leaves and is going to show both to you.

As you are reading this lesson, if you don't have leaves in your yard right now, just read through and remember this information for later. In the fall, when there are leaves around you can put this information into practice.

If you have a lawn mower and a leaf blower use these directions.

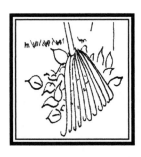

Step 1. Using your leaf blower, blow all the leaves around the edge of your yard into the middle area.

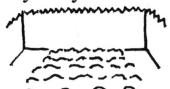

Step 2. Mow all the leaves up with your lawn mower, making sure to catch them in the mower's bag.

Step 3. Empty mower's bag as needed into large, black lawn bags. Take to dump or make into compost.

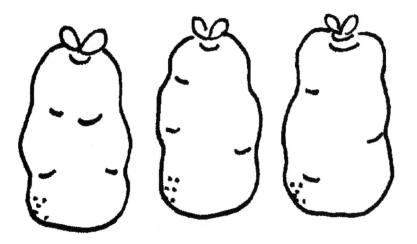

If you only have a rake use these directions.

Step 1. Start at one corner of your yard and work around in a circle. Rake the edges of your lawn, making sure to bag the piles of leaves a you go.

Step 2. Have a brother or sister hold the bags as you put the piled leaves in them. If you don't have someone to help, put the plastic bag in a large, empty garbage can and fill it as you go. Once the bag is filled, tie securely.

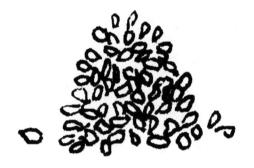

Step 3. After all the edges are clean, start working your way around the yard making piles. After you make six piles, bag them and keep going until the job is finished.

Prayer: (In your own words.) Thank the Lord for the four seasons He has created. Thank Him for His wonderful creation and how He made the trees to hibernate in winter and come alive again in the Spring.

TASK: If you have leaves around your house that need to be taken care of, do this job this week. If you don't, remember this information for when the leaves start to fall. You may be able to earn some money by raking leaves in your neighborhood!

That you might walk worthy of the Lord unto all pleasing, being
fruitful in every good work, and increasing in the knowledge of God.
Colossians 1:10

Week Twenty-four

Responsibility & How to Water the Lawn

Josh is responsible for watering his lawn. This is a very important job, for if he does it wrong, his grass could die.

Have you ever watered your lawn before? It's easy to just turn on a sprinkler and let the water get the lawn wet, but did you know that there is much more to watering a lawn than that?

Your lawn is made up of grass, a plant. Like any plant, they need special care and food, just like one of your Mom's house plants, if she has any. In this lesson we are going to learn the correct way to water the lawn.

1. *When do you start watering your lawn?* You start to water when the first Spring rains start. The rains cause your grass to come out of dormancy (they have been sleeping all winter). If you don't water them after the rains start, it drains their food reserves and you won't have a healthy lawn.

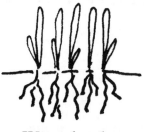

Water deeply

2. *How often do you water your lawn?* If your lawn has been there for a long time, you need to only water twice a week. You do have to make sure that you have watered thoroughly, so that the moisture gets down to the roots of the grass.

3. *How much water does your lawn need?* For cool season grasses, they need about one and a half inches of water each week.

3. *When do you water your lawn?* You need to water your lawn in the early morning while it is cool. Do not water in the afternoon because the water evaporates away and is a waste of time and water. Do not water at night because it can increase your lawn's chance for diseases.

4. *How can you help to conserve water?* You can mow your lawn a bit higher. This means to leave the lawn a bit longer. Don't mow it so closely to the ground.

Prayer: (In your own words.) Thank God for giving you the grass to run around on in your bare feet. Ask Him for His strength and wisdom as you tend the grass and garden just like Adam did in the beginning of time.

TASK: Discuss with your Dad when he wants you to water the lawn and how he would like it to be done. Plan out on a calendar the days that you will water and figure out how much time it takes to water 1 1/2 inches.

Stay on top of the task and make sure to have your Dad check how you are doing so that he can correct anything. Soon you will be able to water the lawn all by yourself!

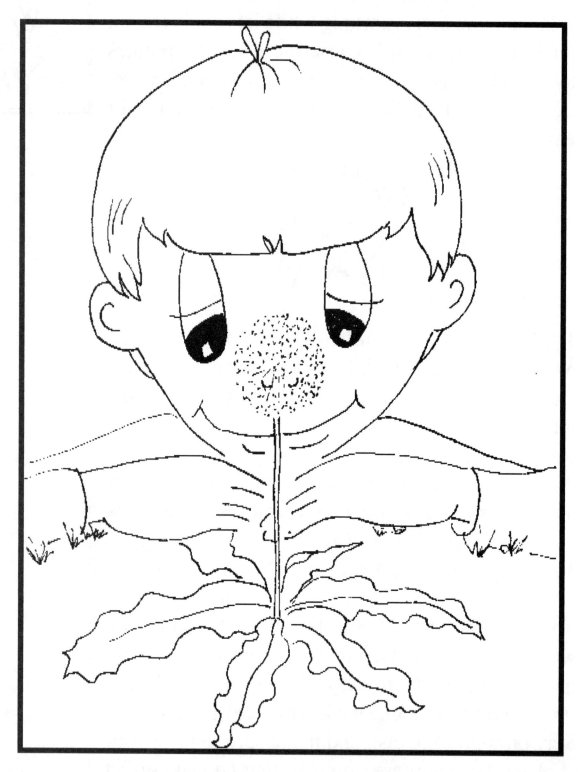

For even when we were with you, this we commanded you, that if
any would not work, neither should he eat.
2 Thessalonians 3:10

Week Twenty-Five

Responsible in Strength

Responsibility & How to Weed

You will notice while you are watering your lawn, that some funny looking yellow flowers may be sprouting up all over. These are called Dandelions, and while some people like to cultivate them and eat them as greens, most people look at them as fast spreading weeds!

Have you ever weeded before? Josh has decided to earn some extra money in his neighborhood by weeding for them. Weeding is not necessarily an easy job. There are some things you need to know and weeds you need to learn to identify.

In this lesson, we are going to learn to identify common weeds that are found in most lawns and gardens, and then learn how to get rid of them so that they never come back!

Weed 1: *This plant is the common Dandelion.* It's roots grow very deep into the ground. You need a Dandelion tool to help dig deep in the ground and twist around its roots. In order to get rid of the Dandelion you must remove every bit of root or else it will sprout again. Once removed, shake some grass seeds in its spot to cover the bare ground.

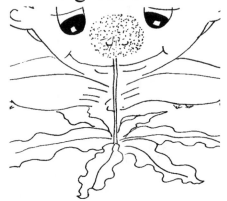

Weed 2: *This plant is Clover.* It is found in most gardens and doesn't do much damage. It is hazardous if you have small children running around barefoot because the bees are attracted to it. Many children are stung each year because of stepping on the clover in the yard. Simply pull the clover out by hand. Shake grass seed on the empty spot.

Weed 3: *Thistle Sprouts.* These are the prickly weeds that stick small needles into your hands or gloves

when you try to pull them out. Remove these weeds the same as you would Dandelions.

Weed 4: *Morning Glories.* Morning Glories come back year after year. You must get the roots but any pieces that are left will sprout again. If you ask your Dad to rototill the area where they are found, this can hurt its food reserves and finally allow grass to grow.

Prayer: (In your own words.) Thank God for even the weeds. You know why they got there and soon we will be in Heaven where there will be no weeds.

TASK: Discuss with your parents where and when they would like you to weed. Read Genesis 3:17-19

And when you liest down, you shall not be afraid; yes, you shall lie down, and your sleep shall be sweet.
Proverbs 3:24

Week Twenty-Six

Responsible in Strength

Responsibility & Learning to "Fix" Things

Josh recently read a book which told him that at sometime, everything on earth will break. It's a given. As a young man, God has created you in the image of Him. God is creative. He creates, he fixes, he imagines... You also have these traits within you.

Have you ever heard of a "Mr. Fix it"? Mr. Fix It is a nickname given to men who are capable of fixing things themselves rather than having to throw items away because they are broken.

When you grow up you probably are going to be a husband and dad. You will also have a house that you will be taking care of and all the things that go into a house. You are going to have to be *Mr. Fix It* for your own family!

How do you become a *Mr. Fix It*, you ask? By starting now. You need to start fixing everything that you break. Get it into your mind that in most cases you can fix it.

What can you fix right now at your age? Here are some suggestions. With the help of your Dad you should be able to put together just about any of the following:

1. A broken piece of china
2. A book that has lost its cover
3. A tear in your pants
4. A broken rake handle
5. A Lego toy that has been taken apart and all you have is the picture. You can do it!
6. A flat bicycle tire
7. Slow wheels on a skateboard
8. A broken fence
9. A dent in some furniture
10. A broken shelf

Can you think of some things that you have already fixed? I bet there are plenty of things that you can do. Josh has even fixed his parents computer! He knew more about disc cleaning than they did.

One of the main things about fixing things is knowing about how they work. This is why science is so much fun. Science teaches us how things work and why. When you get a bit older you can learn in science

how to make a radio, a lightbulb work on a battery and much more! These things wil help you to be able to fix things around your house when you are older and even now.

Prayer: (In your own words.) Thank our Father for all of His creation and for His great mysteries. Ask Him to give you an inquisitive mind so that you will be able to take things apart and then put them back together correctly.

TASK: If you have access to the Internet, with your parent/s at your side, go to www.howstuffworks.com. This is a great web site. It tells you how everything works. For example, once you are at this site,

1. Click on Home Stuff.
2. Click on How Batteries Work
3. Click on the Next Page to go to article

Right there you have great pictures and information which tell you exactly how a battery works.

There are thousands of things to look up. There is another interesting item whose caption was, "what was it like in the Garden of Eden?", and you click on rain forest.

If you do not have a home computer, you might like to visit your local library and use their computer.

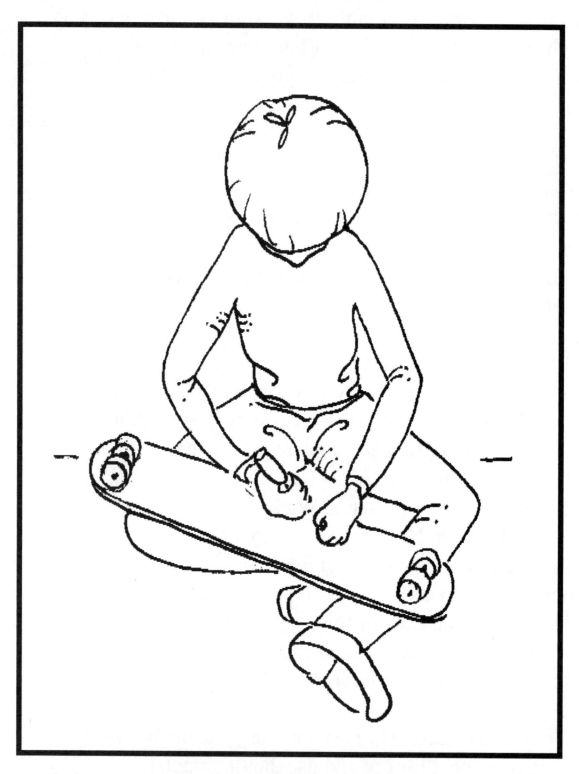

He that keeps the commandments keepeth his own soul;
but he that despises His ways shall die.
Proverbs 19:16

Week Twenty-Seven

Responsibility & Fixing a Slow Skateboard

Josh loves to skateboard. He skateboards outside in front of his home, at skate parks, anywhere where it is allowed.

Because he skateboards so much, his skateboard has become very slow. Instead of throwing his skateboard away, his Dad told him that he could easily fix it himself.

So Josh and Dad went to their nearest skateboard shop and asked the salesman what they could do. The solution was easy. You can do it too! You just need to ask your Dad if he will help you.

Fixing a Slow Skateboard

Caution! You need your parent/s to help you do this. Ammonia is toxic and dangerous. Let Dad do the ammonia part.

Step 1. Remove the nut holding each wheel in place with a wrench.

Step 2. In the middle of each wheel are bearings. There is one on each side. With a screwdriver take out both bearings from each wheel. Just insert the tip of the screwdriver into the center of the bearing and pop it out.

Step 3. Clean the bearings with a clean rag.

Step 4. Drop the bearings into a cup of ammonia and let them soak there for one hour and a half.

Step 5. Remove the bearings and rinse off the ammonia with water. Spin them and make sure they are completely dry.

Step 6. Now soak the bearings in a cup of motor oil overnight.

Step 7. In the morning, take them out of the oil and dry them off with a clean rag.

Step 8. Pop them back into the wheels and replace the wheels on the skateboard. Do not overtighten the wheel nuts.

Step 9. You're ready to ROLL!

Prayer: (In your own words.) Thank your Heavenly Father for allowing you to have a skateboard and other items that are for play. Ask Him to keep you safe and to teach you to obey the safety rules of skateboarding.

TASK: This week try to fix your skateboard with your dad. If you don't have a slow skateboard, ask one of your friends if you can make his board go faster. I'm sure that he won't mind!

Pray without ceasing.
1 Thessalonians 5:17

Week Twenty-Eight

Responsibility & Fixing a Bicycle Tire

Josh knows that he won't be able to drive a car until he is older. Now the fastest way for him to get to his friend's house is with his bicycle. Because he does ride his bike a lot, he tends to get flat tires often.

His Dad knew this was going to happen and so he got him all set up with everything he was going to need. Do you ride your bicycle very often? Have you ever had a flat tire yet? It is very easy to fix a flat tire. All you need to do is to know the right size of your tire and have the correct tools. With Dad's help it will be a breeze.

How to Change a Flat Bicycle Tire

Dad will need to help you with this at first. You will need to buy the bicycle tire tools or levers, a new inner tube, a patch kit, and a bicycle pump.

.

Step 1. You need to remove the wheel from your bike by releasing the lever on each axle. Just flip up one of the levers to loosen the wheel and then you can just pull it out.

Step 2. If this is an older bike you will have to loosen the two axle nuts holding the wheels in place with a wrench. The wheels will then come out.

Step 3. Deflate the tire.

Step 4. Use a tire tool and glide it between the rim and the tire. You are going to pry the tire away from the rim all the way around. Do this again with another tire tool and make sure the other side comes free.

Step 5. Remove the inner tube and the tire from the rim.

Step 6. Inflate the inner tube and find where the holes are by listening for the "hiss".

Step 7. Once you have found your hole apply glue

to both the inner tube and the rubber patch. Count to 20 before pressing the patch onto the hole. Let dry for at least ten minutes.

Step 8. Put a little bit of air in the inner tube to check to see if it is still leaking. If it is fine, put the fixed tube back into the tire.

Step 9. Now you are going to put the tire back onto the rim. Find the hole in the rim for the inflation tube and pull the valve through the hole and pull the tire over the wheel.

Step 10. Push one side of the tire onto the rim with your fingers. The tire will want to go around the inside edge of the rim.

Step 11. Now that you have one side on the rim, check that everything is smooth and that there are no kinks.

Step 12. Go to the other side of the wheel and with your fingers, again, push the other side of the tire onto the rim. It may be difficult to push the remaining piece of tire in, but you can do it.

Step 13. Now you can reinflate the tire to it's normal pressure level.

You've done it!

Enter into His gates with thanksgiving, and into His courts with praise. Be thankful unto Him and bless His name!
Psalms 100:4

Week Twenty-Nine

Responsible in Soul

Responsibility & Being Your Dad's Shadow

God has given you a great gift when He gave you your Dad. Your Dad was once just like you. He was young, liked to play, had his good friends, his favorite candy, and liked to hug and kiss his Mother at night before he went to bed.

Someday you are going to be like your Dad. You are going to grow up strong and tall, just like he is.

One way to learn how to be responsible is to watch all that your Dad does. Think about what a great man he is. He works, he takes care of his family, he brings home the money he earns and buys food for you to eat. Your Dad is a hero. He loves his family and he loves you!

Books and curriculum are great ways to learn how to

My Dad is My HERO

do things. They can teach us an awful lot. But one of the best ways to learn about being a responsible gentleman is by walking alongside your Dad when you can.

The Bible tells us that Dads are to teach God's ways to their children, speaking of them when they are sitting in their house, and when they walk by the way, when they lie down, and when they get up. Deuteronomy 11:19

Did you know that God's Word tells us that Dads are to be teaching their children the minute that you are no longer nursing or drinking from a bottle?

"Whom shall he teach knowledge? and whom shall he make to understand doctrine? Them that are weaned from the milk. For precept must be upon precept, precept upon precept; line upon line, line upon line, here a little and there a little." Isaiah 28:9-10

What does it mean to be taught precept upon precept? Think of how you are learning to do your math. What was the first thing you learned? You first learned how to count. The next thing you learned was what the numbers you were counting looked like. The following thing was to learn to add $1 + 1 = 2$. And from there you took off!

The same thing goes for responsibility. You are learning as you grow. Each year you will learn to do new and more difficult tasks. You will be responsible for more and more, and the more you are responsible, the more your parents and others will trust you.

You need to take time to talk with your Dad.
Watch how he shaves,
Watch how he talks to your Mom,
Watch how he reads the Bible,
Watch how he teaches his children,
Watch how he talks to other men,
Keep your eyes on your Dad. He is reflecting Christ. The Bible says that Christ is his head, or leader.

We all know that sometimes our Dads may not be perfect. It is your duty to pray for your father and mother. Your Dad is God's child too, and God is still training him up until the day that Jesus comes or when the Lord brings your Dad home.

Prayer: (In your own words.) Thank your Father God for the Dad and Mom that He has given you. Ask the Lord to help you to learn all the great things that your Dad has to teach you, and that you will have a teachable and willing spirit.

TASK: This week make an appointment with your Dad and ask him to teach you some things that he thinks you need to know. Ask him if he will teach you the Bible and tell you the things that you need to learn from it. If he can, maybe you can have a weekly Bible study with your Dad. Just you gentlemen!

Continue in prayer, and watch in the same with thanksgiving.
Colossians 4:2

Week Thirty

Responsible in Soul

Review & Putting it All Into Practice

Can you believe that this is the last week in your book? You have sure worked hard. Do you feel like you have become more responsible? I'll bet that even your parents are looking at you differently now. You can do so many things.

Now that you have finished the book, it's important that you remember what you have learned. In this last lesson, let's go over some of the topics and see if you can remember things from previous lessons.

Before we do this, let's read this Scripture one more time:

"But be ye doers of the Word, and not hearers only, deceiving your own selves." James 1:22

Congratulations!

Questions for Review

1. What does "responsible" mean? (Pg. 7)

2. What relationship should be number one in your life? (Pg.11)

3. If you call out to God, does He hear you and will He answer you? (Pg.12-13)

4. What is your armour that you put on? (Pg.16)

5. What is your only defense against the enemy? (Pg. 16 & 17)

6. Why is the Word of God called the Sword of the Spirit? (Pg. 16 & 17)

7. What is the meaning of "fellowship"? (Pg. 20)

8. How do you let your light shine? (Pg. 24)

9. How does a gentleman behave? (Pg. 28)

10. Is he "clownish"? (Pg. 28)

11. Give some ways in which you can show consideration for others? (Pg. 32)

12. What should you say when you answer the telephone? (Pg. 35)

13. How would you introduce a new person at church to your friends? (Pg. 40)

14. Can you name some things that you shouldn't ever talk about with other people? (Pg. 45)

15. Can you remember the suggestions regarding what you should do to show you are listening to someone? (Pg. 49)

16. What does it mean to be "self-centered"? (Pg. 52)

Congratulations!

17. What is a "first impression"? (Pg. 55)

18. What should you wear to a wedding or a funeral? (Pg. 60)

19. Name one of the six questions that you should ask yourself as you dress. (Pg. 62)

20. What are four things that you should keep groomed? (Pg. 68)

21. What is a good steward? What is a bad steward? (Pg. 72)

22. What is a "give me heart"? (Pg 76)

23. What are the rich supposed to do in this life? (Pg. 80)

24. Describe a sloth. (Pg. 83)

25. Name some of the rules that you should follow if you want to be a hard worker. (Pg. 85)

26. Explain how your money can grow, even though it doesn't grow on trees. (Pg. 88)

27. Please list some of the responsibilities that you have around your home. (Pg. 92)

28. Describe how you would rake the leaves in your yard. (Pg. 96)

29. What time of day should you water your lawn, and how much water should you give it? (Pg.100)

30. Which is the worst weed to pull out? (Pg. 104)

31. Do you remember the web address for the website that tells you how things work? (Pg. 108)

32. On this earth, who is your example of manhood? (Pg. 119)

33. Who should you shadow? (Pg.120)

Read the Bible Through in One Year

Month 1	Month 2	Month 3	Month 4
1 = Genesis 1-3	1 = Leviticus 1-4	1 = Deuteronomy 5-7	1 = 1 Samuel 11-13
2 = Genesis 4-7	2 = Leviticus 5-7	2 = Deuteronomy 8-10	2 = 1 Samuel 14, 15
3 = Genesis 8-11	3 = Leviticus 8, 9	3 = Deuteronomy 11-13	3 = 1 Samuel 16, 17
4 = Genesis 12-15	4 = Leviticus 10-12	4 = Deuteronomy 14-17	4 = 1 Samuel 18-20
5 = Genesis 16-18	5 = Leviticus 13	5 = Deuteronomy 18-20	5 = 1 Samuel 21-24
6 = Genesis 19-20	6 = Leviticus 14, 15	6 = Deuteronomy 21-23	6 = 1 Samuel 25-27
7 = Genesis 21-23	7 = Leviticus 16-18	7 = Deuteronomy 24-26	7 = 1 Samuel 28-31
8 = Genesis 24, 25	8 = Leviticus 19-21	8 = Deuteronomy 27, 28	8 = 2 Samuel 1-3
9 = Genesis 26-28	9 = Leviticus 22, 23	9 = Deuteronomy 29-31	9 = 2 Samuel 4-7
10 = Genesis 29, 30	10 = Leviticus 24, 25	10 = Deuteronomy 32-34	10 = 2 Samuel 8-11
11 = Genesis 31, 32	11 = Leviticus 26, 27	11 = Joshua 1-4	11 = 2 Samuel 12, 13
12 = Genesis 33-35	12 = Numbers 1-2	12 = Joshua 5-7	12 = 2 Samuel 14, 15
13 = Genesis 36-38	13 = Numbers 3, 4	13 = Joshua 8, 9	13 = 2 Samuel 16, 17
14 = Genesis 39-41	14 = Numbers 5, 6	14 = Joshua 10, 11	14 = 2 Samuel 18, 19
15 = Genesis 42-44	15 = Numbers 7	15 = Joshua 12-14	15 = 2 Samuel 20-22
16 = Genesis 45-47	16 = Numbers 8-10	16 = Joshua 15-17	16 = 2 Samuel 23, 24
17 = Genesis 48-50	17 = Numbers 11-13	17 = Joshua 18-20	17 = 1 Kings 1
18 = Exodus 1-3	18 = Numbers 14, 15	18 = Joshua 21, 22	18 = 1 Kings 2, 3
19 = Exodus 4-6	19 = Numbers 16-18	19 = Joshua 23, 24	19 = 1 Kings 4-6
20 = Exodus 7-9	20 = Numbers 19-21	20 = Judges 1-3	20 = 1 Kings 7
21 = Exodus 10-12	21 = Numbers 22-24	21 = Judges 4-6	21 = 1 Kings 8
22 = Exodus 13-15	22 = Numbers 25, 26	22 = Judges 7, 8	22 = 1 Kings 9, 10
23 = Exodus 16-18	23 = Numbers 27-29	23 = Judges 9, 10	23 = 1 Kings 11, 12
24 = Exodus 19-21	24 = Numbers 30, 31	24 = Judges 11-13	24 = 1 Kings 13, 14
25 = Exodus 22-24	25 = Numbers 32, 33	25 = Judges 14-16	25 = 1 Kings 15-17
26 = Exodus 25-27	26 = Numbers 34-36	26 = Judges 17-19	26 = 1 Kings 18, 19
25 = Exodus 28, 29	27 = Deuteronomy 1, 2	27 = Judges 20, 21	27 = 1 Kings 20, 21
28 = Exodus 30-32	28 = Deuteronomy 3, 4	28 = Ruth 1-4	28 = 1 Kings 22, 2 Ki. 1
29 = Exodus 33-35	. . .	29 = 1 Samuel 1-3	29 = 2 Kings 2-4
30 = Exodus 36-38	. . .	30 = 1 Samuel 4-7	30 = 2 Kings 5-7
31 = Exodus 39, 40	. . .	31 = 1 Samuel 8-10	. . .

Lessons in Responsibility

Month 5	Month 6	Month 7	Month 8
1 = 2 Kings 8, 9	**1** = Ezra 9, 10	**1** = Psalms 90-97	**1** = Isaiah 43-47
2 = 2 Kings 10-12	**2** = Nehemiah 1-3	**2** = Psalm 98-104	**2** = Isaiah 48-51
3 = 2 Kings 13, 14	**3** = Nehemiah 4-6	**3** = Psalms 105-107	**3** = Isaiah 52-56
4 = 2 Kings 15, 16	**4** = Nehemiah 7, 8	**4** = Psalms 108-116	**4** = Isaiah 57-59
5 = 2 Kings 17, 18	**5** = Nehemiah 9,10	**5** = Psalms 117-119:72	**5** = Isaiah 60-63
6 = 2 Kings 19, 21	**6** = Nehemiah 11-13	**6** = Psalms 119:73-176	**6** = Isaiah 64-66
7 = 2 Kings 22-25	**7** = Esther 1-3	**7** = Psalms 120-135	**7** = Jeremiah 1-3
8 = 1 Chronicles 1	**8** = Esther 4-7	**8** = Psalms 136-142	**8** = Jeremiah 4-6
9 = 1 Chronicles 2-4	**9** = Esther 8-10	**9** = Psalms 143-150	**9** = Jeremiah 7-9
10 = 1 Chronicles 5, 6	**10** = Job 1-5	**10** = Proverbs 1-4	**10** = Jeremiah 10-12
11 = 1 Chronicles 7-9	**11** = Job 6-10	**11** = Proverbs 5-8	**11** = Jeremiah 13-15
12 = 1 Chronicles 10-12	**12** = Job 11-15	**12** = Proverbs 9-13	**12** = Jeremiah 16-18
13 = 1 Chronicles 13-16	**13** = Job 16-21	**13** = Proverbs 14-17	**13** = Jeremiah 19-22
14 = 1 Chronicles 17-19	**14** = Job 22-28	**14** = Proverbs 18-21	**14** = Jeremiah 23-25:16
15 = 1 Chronicles 20-23	**15** = Job 29-33	**15** = Proverbs 22-24	**15** = Jeremiah 25:17-27
16 = 1 Chronicles 24-26	**16** = Job 34-37	**16** = Proverbs 25-28	**16** = Jeremiah 28-30
17 = 1 Chronicles 27-29	**17** = Job 38-42	**17** = Proverbs 29-31	**17** = Jeremiah 31, 32
18 = 2 Chronicles 1-4	**18** = Psalms 1-9	**18** = Ecclesiastes 1-6	**18** = Jeremiah 33-35
19 = 2 Chronicles 5-7	**19** = Psalms 10-17	**19** = Ecclesiastes 7-12	**19** = Jeremiah 36-38
20 = 2 Chronicles 8-10	**20** = Psalms 18-22	**20** = Song / Solomon 1-8	**20** = Jeremiah 39-41
21 = 2 Chronicles 11-14	**21** = Psalms 23-31	**21** = Isaiah 1-4	**21** = Jeremiah 42-44
22 = 2 Chronicles 15-18	**22** = Psalms 32-37	**22** = Isaiah 5-8	**22** = Jeremiah 45-48
23 = 2 Chronicles 19-22	**23** = Psalms 38-44	**23** = Isaiah 9-12	**23** = Jeremiah 49, 50
24 = 2 Chronicles 23-25	**24** = Psalms 45-51	**24** = Isaiah 13-16	**24** = Jeremiah 51, 52
25 = 2 Chronicles 26-28	**25** = Psalms 52-59	**25** = Isaiah 17-21	**25** = Lamentations 1, 2
26 = 2 Chronicles 29, 30	**26** = Psalms 60-67	**26** = Isaiah 22-25	**26** = Lamentations 3-5
27 = 2 Chronicles 31-33	**27** = Psalms 68-71	**27** = Isaiah 26-28	**27** = Ezekiel 1-4
28 = 2 Chronicles 34, 35	**28** = Psalms 72-77	**28** = Isaiah 29-31	**28** = Ezekiel 5-8
29 = 2 Chron. 36, Ezra 1, 2	**29** = Psalms 78-81	**29** = Isaiah 32-35	**29** = Ezekiel 9-12
30 = Ezra 3-5	**30** = Psalms 82-89	**30** = Isaiah 36-38	**30** = Ezekiel 13-15
31 = Ezra 6-8	. . .	**31** = Isaiah 39-42	**31** = Ezekiel 16

Lessons in Responsibility

Month 9	Month 10	Month 11	Month 12
1 = Ezekiel 17-19	**1** = Zechariah 11-14	**1** = Luke 21, 22	**1** = 1 Corinthians 12-14
2 = Ezekiel 20, 21	**2** = Malachi 1-4	**2** = Luke 23, 24	**2** = 1 Corinthians 15, 16
3 = Ezekiel 22, 23	**3** = Matthew 1-4	**3** = John 1-3	**3** = 2 Corinthians 1-4
4 = Ezekiel 24-26	**4** = Matthew 5, 6	**4** = John 4, 5	**4** = 2 Corinthians 5-8
5 = Ezekiel 27, 28	**5** = Matthew 7-9	**5** = John 6, 7	**5** = 2 Corinthians 9-13
6 = Ezekiel 29-31	**6** = Matthew 10-12	**6** = John 8, 9	**6** = Galatians 1-4
7 = Ezekiel 32, 33	**7** = Matthew 13, 14	**7** = John 10, 11	**7** = Gal.5, 6; Eph. 1, 2
8 = Ezekiel 34-36	**8** = Matthew 15-17	**8** = John 12, 13	**8** = Ephesians 3-6
9 = Ezekiel 37, 38	**9** = Matthew 18-20	**9** = John 14-16	**9** = Philippians 1-4
10 = Ezekiel 39, 40	**10** = Matthew 21, 22	**10** = John 17, 18	**10** = Colossians 1-4
11 = Ezekiel 41-43	**11** = Matthew 23, 24	**11** = John 19-21	**11** = 1 Thessalonians 1-4
12 = Ezekiel 44, 45	**12** = Matthew 25, 26	**12** = Acts 1-3	**12** = 1 Thes. 5, 2 Thes. 1-3
13 = Ezekiel 46-48	**13** = Matthew 27, 28	**13** = Acts 4-6	**13** = 1 Timothy 1-4
14 = Daniel 1, 2	**14** = Mark 1-3	**14** = Acts 7, 8	**14** = 1 Timothy 5, 6
15 = Daniel 3, 4	**15** = Mark 4, 5	**15** = Acts 9, 10	**15** = 2 Timothy 1-4
16 = Daniel 5, 6	**16** = Mark 6, 7	**16** = Acts 11-13	**16** = Titus 1-3; Philemon
17 = Daniel 7, 8	**17** = Mark 8, 9	**17** = Acts 14-16	**17** = Hebrews 1-5
18 = Daniel 9, 10	**18** = Mark 10, 11	**18** = Acts 17, 18	**18** = Hebrews 6-9
19 = Daniel 11, 12	**19** = Mark 12, 13	**19** = Acts 19, 20	**19** = Hebrews 10, 11
20 = Hosea 1-6	**20** = Mark 14-16	**20** = Acts 21, 22	**20** = Hebrews 12, 13
21 = Hosea 7-12	**21** = Luke 1	**21** = Acts 23-25	**21** = James 1-5
22 = Hos. 13, 14; Joel 1-3	**22** = Luke 2, 3	**22** = Acts 26-28	**22** = 1 Peter 1-4
23 = Amos 1-5	**23** = Luke 4, 5	**23** = Romans 1-3	**23** = 1 Peter 5; 2 Peter 1-3
24 = Amos 6-9; Obadiah	**24** = Luke 6, 7	**24** = Romans 4-7	**24** = 1 John 1-5
25 = Jonah 1-4, Mic. 1, 2	**25** = Luke 8	**25** = Romans 8-10	**25** = 2 John; 3 John; Jude
26 = Micah 3-7	**26** = Luke 9	**26** = Romans 11-14	**26** = Revelation 1-3
27 = Nahum, Habakkuk	**27** = Luke 10, 11	**27** = Romans 15, 16	**27** = Revelation 4-8
28 = Zephaniah, Haggai	**28** = Luke 12, 13	**28** = 1 Corinthians 1-4	**28** = Revelation 9-12
29 = Zechariah 1-6	**29** = Luke 14-16	**29** = 1 Corinthians 5-8	**29** = Revelation 13-16
30 = Zechariah 7-10	**30** = Luke 17, 18	**30** = 1 Corinthians 9-10	**30** = Revelation 17-19
. . .	**31** = Luke 19, 20	. . .	**31** = Revelation 20-22

Notes

ORDER FORM

___Narrow Way Character Curriculum $32.95
(Includes 8 Pearable Kingdom Stories-Are not repeated in Volumes Below)

Pearables Kingdom Stories:
___ Volume 1 $17.50
___ Volume 2 $17.50
___ Volume 3 $17.50

___Narrow Way Character Curriculum & Pearables 1,2, & 3 Volumes SET (listed above) $72.00

___ Personal Help for Boys Text & Workbook $24.95 (Bound in One Book)

Our Hope Chest Series:

___ Volume 1 - Personal Help for Girls $22.50

___ Volume 2 - Preparing Your Hope Chest $22.50

The Quiet Arts Series, <u>Home Economics for Home Schoolers:</u>

___ Level 1 (Ages 6 and up) $18.95
___ Level 2 (Ages 8 and up) $18.95
___ Level 3 (Ages 10 and up) $18.95

___ALL three Levels of Home Economics $45

The Gentleman's Series, <u>Training in Responsibility</u>

___ Level 1 (Ages 6 and up) $18.95
___ Level 2 (Ages 8 and up) $18.95

___Subtotal
___ Shipping (Please add $3 for orders under $30. $30 & over please add 10%. Out of U.S. please add 25% of total.)

Name_____

Address_____

City/St/Zip_____

Please mail your purchase order to:

PEARABLES
P.O. Box 1071
Mukilteo, WA 98275

Visit **www.pearables.com** for samples and FREE SHIPPING online.